All About
Amelia Earhart

Lew Freedman

BLUE RIVER PRESS

Indianapolis, Indiana

Contents

Amelia loved nothing more than flying

All About
Amelia Earhart

Preface

Amelia Earhart was a pioneer pilot, an aviator who was the best-known and most popular female flyer of her time. She established many records in the early days of flight.

She was born in Atchison, Kansas in 1897, and grew up in a time period when piloting was mostly for men. It took great skill and courage to zoom up into the unknown sky, and Amelia exhibited both of those traits. Earhart would grow into a successful woman who would capture the attention and admiration of all Americans as well as citizens around the world.

Her flying adventures in the 1920s and 1930s were very dramatic because the lightweight planes she flew were still being developed and improved upon. In fact, very few people flew anywhere to travel between cities. Instead they drove or rode the trains since they were thought to be safer. The United States, at that time, was just learning how to fly airplanes and how to enhance other ways of travel like automobiles and trains.

Pilots such as Earhart were treated as heroes as they established new records for flying. They made records for how many hours they flew in the air and how far they flew. Earhart was the first woman to fly across the Atlantic Ocean. She completed this feat alongside pilots Bill Stultz and Louis Gordon in 1928. It was very courageous of her and she received fame and honors for the accomplishment. Later, Earhart gained even greater fame around the world—and more medals and awards—for becoming the first woman to fly solo, or alone, across the Atlantic Ocean in 1932.

During her life, Earhart accomplished things outside of aviation also. She was a generous social worker, a best-selling author, a fashion designer, a college educator, and a lifelong promoter of the rights of women and girls. She always encouraged women—who, during her lifetime, were held back by gender traditions and laws—to find their own careers and specialties, to take charge of their own lives, and to never be discouraged by people who wished to prevent them from chasing their dreams.

In 1937, Earhart and her flight navigator disappeared during an attempted flight around-the-world. They had flown more than 22,000 miles and only had 5,000 more miles left to go. Neither Earhart nor her navigator Fred Noonan were ever seen or heard from again. It is believed their plane crashed in the Pacific Ocean near the Marshall Islands just short of their goal and close to a nearby fuel stop.

They vanished without a trace and long after Earhart's and Noonan's presumed death, experts still wonder what happened to them and why. Though there is no proof about what occurred on July 2, 1937 in the cockpit of the plane, periodic investigations over the decades have been undertaken. Although Amelia Earhart was only thirty-nine years old, she accomplished much and her bravery in the skies has continued to inspire many.

Chapter 1
<u>Growing Up</u>

Amelia Earhart grew up in Kansas. As a little girl, she was never afraid to get dirty climbing fences or playing games with her friends. Part of the time, she and her little sister Muriel, who was two years younger than she, lived with their grandparents in Atchison, Kansas, and part of the time, they lived with their parents in Kansas City, Kansas.

Muriel and Amelia at Muriel's
first birthday party in 1900

Amelia Otis, Amelia Earhart's namesake,
holds her as a baby

Amelia's grandmother, Amelia Otis, often scolded her for not being more ladylike. Yet Amelia's father, Edwin Earhart, always encouraged her to do any activity she wanted to try, even if that meant playing games that typically boys played.

As someone who was born in 1897 and grew up during the early part of the 1900s, Amelia lived during a time when society was not as encouraging of the advancement of women compared to today's standards. Little girls were supposed to wear dresses, not pants. Little girls were supposed to learn how to take care of a house, not play sports.

From the time she was a youngster, Amelia showed signs that she was going to do whatever she wanted to do, even if others did not think that was the proper way for a lady to behave. This outlook, which Amelia maintained for her whole life, enabled her to become a pioneering aviator; to confront unusual challenges, and to always stand up for the rights of women.

Amelia was born in her grandparents' home
in Atchison, Kansas in 1897

When Amelia Mary Earhart was born, she was not born in a hospital, as became common in later years across the United States, but was born in her grandparents' home.

Her grandpa, Alfred Otis, was a judge. For the first three years of Amelia's life, she lived in Kansas City with her mother and her father, who was an attorney.

However, after she turned three years old, Amelia spent the winters of her youth in her grandparents' home fifty miles away in Atchison. Amelia was never attracted to playing with dolls. She chose more active pursuits and adventures outdoors. As a youngster, she was exposed to fishing, bicycling, and basketball. One year she asked for a football for Christmas, which her father provided with some amusement.

Amelia was nicknamed "Millie" when she was a child. Three other girls her age were her closest friends and they all undertook many of these outdoor activities together. They threw mud balls at one another, frolicked on the banks of the Missouri River, and went roller skating.

Her grandparents' house was surrounded by a wrought-iron fence, and when Amelia saw the boys in the neighborhood jumping over fences, she decided she could do that, instead of using the gate, as well. Her grandmother was horrified. But no matter how often Amelia was told that she was not behaving properly, she preferred going over, not around the fence.

If there was any daring adventure in the neighborhood, chances were that Amelia played a part. Once, after seeing a real roller coaster at the St. Louis World's Fair in 1904, Amelia enlisted friends to help her build a mini-roller coaster. And when it was complete, she insisted on taking the first ride. The model did not quite conform to any type of sophisticated model, and sure enough, when Amelia made the inaugural ride, she was flipped head over heels and tumbled to the ground. However, modifications were made, and eventually the little roller coaster worked!

Amelia always displayed a grand imagination. She and some of her closest pals climbed into an empty carriage that was not being used and was not attached to any horses. They pretended it was a magical machine that could take them anywhere they wanted to go. They pretended to be world travelers and drew up maps showing where they were heading. When they mentally arrived in Africa, the carriage was transformed into an elephant. They waved toy guns in the air for protection from imaginary threats such as child-eating lions. Years later Amelia would get to visit many of those places for real.

Taking over an empty carriage, Amelia
and her friends traveled to imaginary places
on marvelous adventures

A popular activity in winter was sledding, but a century ago boys and girls did not use the same types of sleds. Boys lay flat on their sleds and shot down the hills head-first. Girls rode modified sleds where they sat up straight. Amelia ignored this societal standard and went down the hills just as the boys did. One day when she was zooming down lying flat, a junk man steering a horse and cart trotted into her path. The driver did not see Amelia as she sped along and the only reason she avoided serious injury was by guiding her sled between the horse's legs. It was a close call.

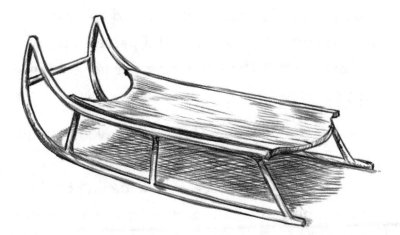

Amelia refused to ride on a girl's sled and chose instead the quick, low sleds the boys used

Many who observed Amelia's bold approach to her activities called her a "tomboy," because she enjoyed participating in what were considered to be boys' activities. Amelia was not insulted; she just shrugged off the characterization.

For much of the 20th century, high school and college sports were available only for boys to compete in, but even in the early years of the century, Amelia had no desire to be pushed to the sidelines as a spectator. A popular new game in the early 1900s was basketball, and one day Amelia approached the captain of the boys' team and asked him to teach her the rules so the girls could play. Amelia learned some of the fundamentals of the sport and passed them on to her friends. Then the girls played amongst themselves in a local park.

While Amelia's grandmother would have preferred that she learn more skills that would be suitable for a housewife, like baking cookies and cleaning the house, Amelia's parents encouraged whatever interests she had. After a few years, her younger sister Muriel joined Amelia in the Atchison-Kansas City living arrangement, and both of them asked dad for a football to play with. He also gave them a small caliber rifle to share, but he had to first reassure Grandma Otis of his decision since guns can be dangerous. The girls would be taught the dangers and how to properly and safely care for it.

Amelia Earhart attended Hyde Park High School in Chicago, Illinois, graduating in 1915

Essentially having two sets of parents (though Amelia was never close to her grandfather) and two homes, the Earhart girls had a pleasant existence. The situation was cut short, however, when their father, Edwin, began having difficulties. He lost various jobs, mostly due to a serious problem with drinking alcohol which made him very sick. Because of his sickness, the family had to move to several cities for new job opportunities including Des Moines, Iowa; St. Paul, Minnesota; Chicago, Illinois; and other cities. Amelia had to attend many schools in these different cities. Because of moving around so much, Amelia's family was very close to each other and tightknit.

Amelia loved her father very much, but the manner in which drinking affected the Earharts' lives deeply affected her. Because her father misused alcohol, he was not reliable or responsible. He could not keep a job or stay focused. Eventually, the family broke down and money became very tight. Although she spent just one year there and hardly made any friends, Amelia graduated from Hyde Park High School in Chicago, Illinois.

An avid reader for most of her life, Amelia was very intelligent, extremely independent, and free-thinking. She was a good candidate to enroll in a top four-year college, but didn't have the funds to enroll anywhere. More importantly, in her mind, she didn't know what she would go to school for. Even as she turned nineteen, after a brief stop at the Ogontz (prep) School in Pennsylvania, Amelia did not know what she wanted to be when she grew up.

Amelia graduates from Ogontz Prep School, a stop between high school and college, in 1918

Many accounts of Earhart's life suggest that she first saw an airplane at the Iowa State Fair in 1908. Others indicate that is not true. The Wright Brothers, Orville and Wilbur, had built the first plane and made the first flight in 1903, some five years earlier and spent the next couple of years developing fixed-wing airplanes.

In any case, in 1908, it was not a routine event for little girls, or any Americans, to glance up at the sky and watch an airplane soar overhead. Today we can look up at the sky and wave to airplanes that are traveling from city to city much more often than Amelia could. In her time, it was extremely rare.

Chapter 2
<u>Finding Wings</u>

Amelia Earhart had blonde hair cut short, grey eyes, freckles, and stood five foot eight. That made her tall for a woman of her time. She was long-legged, almost always photographed wearing slacks, and seemed even taller than she measured.

Amelia, in her signature leather flying jacket and slacks, stands in front of her plane in 1937

One of her appeals was her curly hair, which most people thought was natural. But one of her secrets was that she had to work at keeping it curly.

Not that many people cared how Amelia appeared in public in 1917, a time when she was known only to a small circle of friends and family and she appeared to be on a rather normal path. Amelia and her sister were always close, but frequently separated by distance. That year, Muriel was attending school in Toronto, Canada, and Amelia went there to spend the Christmas holidays.

Restless as she sought a way to make a mark on society, Earhart's life took a dramatic turn that year on her trip to Toronto. Due to encounters with wounded Canadian flyers at a nearby airbase, she found life purpose working as a volunteer nurse treating soldiers injured in World War I. Amelia took first aid courses and nursing courses and served at two hospitals. Ever the adventurer, she was fascinated watching the airplanes take off and land at the nearby airbase.

Generous with her time and money through-out her life, Amelia was raised to be sympathetic to the needy. She enthusiastically responded to the war-ravaged returning soldiers and this service prompted her to consider studying to become a doctor. The experience of helping young, injured soldiers in war was rewarding and beneficial to Amelia. Attending school in Pennsylvania and sitting at a desk seemed silly in comparison. She decided she wanted a career that would be important, have purpose, and be significant to people.

Amelia began working as a nurse in a military hospital during World War I

Almost at the same time as World War I ended, the Great Influenza, or flu, Pandemic of 1918 and 1919 began. It is estimated that this was one of the worst health crises in history, killing more than twenty million people worldwide and 675,000 in the United States. There was no medicinal remedy to combat the illness at the time. Treating hospitalized veterans when the flu struck, Amelia was exposed to illness. She became seriously ill with a bacterial infection and had sinus surgery.

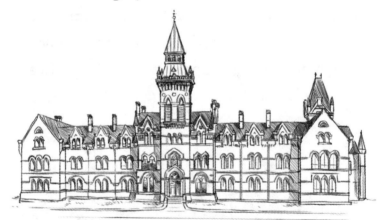

Spadina Military Hospital, where Amelia worked, tried to help those sick with influenza

Amelia's recovery was long and difficult, and she left Canada to rest in Northampton, Massachusetts, where her mother and sister were living. Around that time, her parents reconciled and decided to live together again. So

Amelia moved to Los Angeles, California with her parents in the summer of 1920.

After being seriously sick and having surgery, Amelia moved in with her mother and sister in 1919

California was a hotbed for flying when Amelia moved to the West, even though it was still the pioneering days of airplane use. The machines had improved tremendously in quality and stability from the Wright brothers' first invention. Yet they did not come close to comparing to the planes that began ferrying passengers across the country in the 1930s. Early planes were small, lightweight, fragile vehicles with unreliable engines.

During the 1920s, being a pilot was just about the riskiest job a person could have. There were actually very few jobs for pilots—the United States Postal Service hired a few dozen to deliver the mail. Mostly pilots were adventurers, testing the boundaries of flight and the modernization of the planes. There was a high death rate for both experimental and professional government pilots due to crashes. Even though the planes only traveled at a speed between 75 and 150 miles per hour (mph), much slower than the 500 or 600 mph jets today, there were still lots of dangers. In some cases, the slower speeds did allow pilots who crashed to walk away from their disasters. But during the first part of the decade, parachutes had not even been invented.

A lot of airfields were being built in California, and again Amelia was intrigued by flight. There seemed to be as many airfields as there were movie theatres. Pilot achievements made the news seemingly every day. Air shows were conducted regularly near Amelia's home. Bold pilots flew loops with their single-engine planes, making crowds *ooh* and *ahh*. Amelia was swept up in the craze, thrilled at the sight of pilots making their daring moves in the air.

Amelia became a regular attendee at air shows. That naturally led her to seek a ride. A short flight thrilled her, and she wanted to take

Amelia was trained by another pioneering female pilot, Neta Snook, who owned her own aviation school and agreed to train Amelia on credit

flying lessons. Amelia felt she would gain more from a female instructor and found Neta Snook, an accomplished female pilot. No one knew at the time, but the historic first flying lesson for Amelia Earhart took place on January 3, 1921, at Kinner Airport in Southern California.

Amelia observed the attire of pilots and did her best to wear what she felt was a proper wardrobe. She appeared in her horseback riding outfit since it seemed the most similar. Amelia bought a leather flyer's jacket to wear on top of her horseback outfit. To make the jacket less crisp, she slept in it for a few nights. The jacket then seemed to have more miles on it. All pilots wore goggles and leather helmets at that time too.

Amelia earned her wings in a Curtiss JN-4 "Jenny." The plane was a biplane, which means it had double sets of wings. It had one engine, no door, and two open cockpits.

It weighed just over 1,400 pounds. This particular model was called a "Canuck." The pilot Neta Snook and co-pilot Earhart had to climb over the side of the plane to sit down and were exposed to the forces of the weather as they flew. They could feel the air on their faces and wind in their hair. First built in 1915, the propeller-driven "Jenny" was a major asset to the United States during World War I and was regularly used in the transition from war-time to civilian flight. In general, the "Jenny" did not fly faster than 75 mph.

Amelia's first flight was in a unstable Curtiss JN-4 biplane in 1921

Instantly excited and enthralled at taking the controls of the plane, Amelia was all in for as many lessons as she could get from Snook. Her biggest problem was figuring out how to pay for the lessons. She cut a deal with the teacher for credit, so she could keep up the pace of her learning. Nonetheless, she still had to raise five hundred dollars quickly.

Despite being called a tomboy, Amelia curled her hair to show off her feminine side

For her active lifestyle and her flying lessons, it was practical that Amelia keep her hair short and wear slacks instead of dresses. Still, she did not want to be perceived as lacking femininity or looking too out of the ordinary. That's why she took particular care with her "bobbed" hair and made it flatteringly curly.

Amelia learned aviation quickly, and before the end of the summer, she wanted to purchase her own plane. Amelia did not have a bank account that would support buying even the cheapest of planes. Flying was just about the most expensive hobby a young person could have, and Amelia did not yet have a job.

Amelia's parents were always supportive of their intelligent daughter and her passions, so they helped pay $2,000 for a Kinner Airster airplane. Amelia was twenty-four years old and took her first full-time job. She became a mail and file clerk for the phone company to help pay the bills. Those bills were large as she worked to pay off Snook's lessons and to fuel her new toy. The Airster was also a biplane, as many models of the time were, but it was shorter than the "Jenny" and weighed only six hundred pounds.

As a newer plane, the Airster was superior in construction, lightweight thus more efficient, and it had a new kind of engine, one that was air-cooled. Competing companies were swiftly manufacturing better planes, experimenting with new materials and were determined to make the planes safer. Since many of the finest pilots were injured or lost while flying due to terrible accidents, safety was very important.

Amelia's parents pooled their money to buy her a Kinner Airster, her very first plane

Like all pilots who are seized by the pleasure and adventure of flying, Amelia wanted to make her first solo flight as soon as she could. It didn't take long for her to go out on her own. On Amelia's first solo trip, she flew up to 5,000 feet high and calmly landed her plane. She no longer needed help in the cockpit—the sky really was the limit.

Chapter 3
Life Choices

Since she was a teenager, Amelia Earhart had been collecting newspaper and magazine stories and placing them in a scrapbook. They were all about women's achievements.

If Amelia read a story in her local newspaper about a woman founding a business, she cut it out and pasted it in her book. She did the same thing if she read about a woman in another state who was elected to a school board. Amelia did not know what her career should be, but she always knew that she would not be satisfied as a housewife and mother without also participating in the working world. And the stories about these women were inspirational to her.

Over the years, Amelia kept adding to this scrapbook with story after story. She never stopped filling pages with these reports about women's achievements. She never imagined that someday stories written about her accomplishments would be collected and admired in the same way.

Amelia helped campaign and speak out for the women's rights movement

From the time she was a school girl, Amelia was described as someone who marched to the beat of her own drum. She thought for herself rather than blindly following people. Where another young lady might see obstacles, Amelia looked for ways around them. Once she got an idea, she was determined and committed to it and never afraid of challenges.

The early 1920s represented the glamour days of aviation. Amelia Earhart correctly assessed that there was no physical reason why a woman couldn't become a pilot. She stood five foot eight and weighed only 118 pounds, but it did not take tremendous strength or size to steer an airplane. The only thing that stood in the way was the mindset of men who believed women couldn't control a plane. Many people also believed that a woman's place was only in the home.

Once she bought her own airplane, Amelia flew as often as possible. Experience in the cockpit of the airplane was a very important part of becoming an accomplished pilot. Instead of a steering wheel like in a car, there was a navigation stick in the cockpit to control and steer the plane. During the summer of 1922, Amelia set a new altitude record for women of 14,000 feet in her Airster. *The Los Angeles Times* wrote about her. So did aviation newsletters and magazines. She kept clippings of her own stories for her scrapbooks.

Still, the Earhart family suffered financial setbacks. Amelia was still searching for a fulfilling and lucrative career. Although she would have enjoyed becoming a flight instructor like Neta Snook, there were not many secure positions in that field. In 1924 Amelia's parents divorced. Amelia sold her plane and used the money to buy a bright yellow touring car that she called a "canary." She took that car and drove east with her mother.

Amelia sold her plane to buy a bright
yellow 1923 Kissel Speedster

But during her previous stay in California, Amelia had started dating a young man from Massachusetts named Sam Chapman. They got engaged, and Chapman said that he wanted her to give up her adventurous lifestyle and

Sam and Amelia were engaged in 1923,
but Amelia didn't want to settle down like
he did and they soon broke up again

settle down as a housewife with him. Earhart refused to be tied down to one place; she wanted
to continue exploring. Chapman was originally
from a Boston suburb, and it was pleasant for
him to return to the area when Amelia landed a
job in that city as a social worker at the Denison
House, a well-known settlement home that

provided educational and recreational programs for immigrants. Immigrants are people who were not born in this country, but who choose to live here. Settlement homes, like the one Amelia worked at, were very helpful to immigrants because they offered a community of people and support. Often immigrants did not have family in their new country and had to learn the new culture and sometimes language of the United States by themselves. That is why the Denison House was so helpful to them.

Amelia previously had studied briefly at Columbia University in New York, but had not obtained a college degree. She had little training that would immediately qualify her for social work. However, she made a good impression in interviews, had a genuinely generous nature, and when she cared about something, she had boundless energy and enthusiasm. Those characteristics won her the job.

Amelia thrived in this environment. She was an enthusiastic instructor, a caring listener, and a passionate believer in helping people. She felt she was doing important work, and if not for her itch to fly, she may have settled into a lengthy career in this role. Amelia lived at the Denison House where she worked. She remained friends with Chapman for the rest of her life, but she never married him and never really "settled down" the way he would have preferred.

Amelia taught both adults and children at the Denison House where she was a social worker until 1928

The first assignment Amelia undertook was teaching English and citizenship facts to residents whose first language was not English, but a foreign tongue. Her first students were adults. Another early task Amelia took on was taking immigrant children to nearby hospitals for medical treatment. These were not emergency cases and Amelia provided their rides in her fancy yellow car—an experience that must have greatly appealed to the kids. Before too long, Amelia was in charge of the classes for girls ages five to fourteen. She dealt with and related well to children of all nationalities.

This was a very satisfying time in Amelia's life. She had a profession that made her feel useful and important. Amelia's involvement branched out in a number of ways, and she became a very important employee at Denison House. Amelia no longer owned an airplane, but she still sought the opportunity to fly whenever time allowed. In 1927, Amelia combined her two interests when she flew around Boston and tossed flyers out of the aircraft that advertised a carnival to benefit the Denison House.

A new airfield was opening in nearby Quincy, and Amelia's West Coast connections helped her get a job. Her background at Kinner Airport led to part-time work at the airfield, including designing the waiting rooms. For once, Amelia had a large enough income. There was also quick progress occurring in aviation, and she devoured any information about airplanes and pilots. The biggest worldwide news was the stunning first solo flight crossing of the Atlantic Ocean by Charles Lindbergh during May 20 and May 21 in 1927.

Lindbergh instantly became world famous for the achievement, won a cash prize, was rewarded with medals, and ensured his place in history. Some St. Louis businessmen had put up a prize of $25,000 for the first pilot who could fly across the Atlantic Ocean. At the time, Lindbergh was a mail pilot and he was intrigued by the challenge. Flying "The Spirit of St. Louis" plane, Lindbergh completed the 3,500 mile flight from New York to Paris in thirty-three and a half hours. One-by-one, the great prizes in aviation were rewarded, but not to women. The world awaited the first flight across the Atlantic by a woman. Several tried and several died attempting it.

Earhart was well known within the aviation community, but was not a public figure yet. She was a member of the National Aeronautic Association's Boston chapter and gained attention by writing a letter complaining that there was not enough effort given to promoting aviation.

Amelia believed in the future of aviation as commercial transportation, as well as the role women could play in boosting interest in flight. She obtained more attention from the public when she wrote an article about flying for a Boston magazine. This article began to make her into a public figure, known by ordinary citizens.

For the most part, Amelia was just following her instincts and voicing her beliefs. Not only was she a true believer in aviation's future, she wanted to make certain that women were not held back by gender ideas. Amelia wanted both men and women to support the advancement of women's careers and aspirations. She did not agree with the standards of her time that pre-ferred women stay in the home.

By achieving her desire to have a meaningful career and take flight in small planes whenever she could, Amelia had found her calling. What she could not have known was that by voicing her thoughts, sometimes controversially, her life would be changed.

Chapter 4
<u>Historic Flight</u>

Amelia Earhart made a good impression. She did not consider herself to be beautiful, but she was attractive and her ready smile welcomed people and made her seem alluring. She was outgoing and talkative and expressed herself well. Once she established herself as a flyer and as an energetic social worker, her self-confidence shined through.

Earhart, Stultz, and Gordon planned to fly across the Atlantic from Newfoundland to Paris

Various women had attempted to fly across the Atlantic Ocean and had failed. A wealthy woman named Amy Guest was searching for the right female pilot to make the journey. Ever since Charles Lindbergh's historic flight in 1927, the focus was now on if and when a woman would make the journey across the Atlantic.

In 1926, Commander Richard Byrd and Floyd Bennett flew to the North Pole from Spitsbergen, Norway, a distance of 1,535 miles, in fifteen hours and fifty-seven minutes. They spent thirteen minutes flying circles around the Pole before returning to civilization. Byrd was touted as a hero. However, in later years, some people felt they did not actually make it all of the way to their destination.

Amy Guest bought the plane flown at the North Pole by Commander Byrd and intended to fly it to Europe with a crew. She was fifty-five years old, and her family urged her not to try. Instead, she sought out a different pilot to fly the plane and the right woman aviator to be the first across the Atlantic Ocean. She asked a small team to help her find someone. As it turns out, publisher and publicist George P. Putnam was friendly with the group Guest asked and joined the hunt. He was part of the small group of men that interviewed Amelia and decided that she was the best choice to be the female pilot. This was the first time Amelia and George met, but eventually they would become husband and wife.

As the summer of 1928 approached, Amelia was working at the Denison House. She kept the plans for the trip quiet. She intended to take a couple of weeks of vacation for the trans-Atlantic flight and return to work after.

The "Friendship" was equipped with pontoons so that it could take off from and land in water

The airplane, an F7 Fokker with a 225-horse-power engine and four 95-gallon gas tanks on the wings with bonus tanks in the cabin, was named "Friendship." Amy Guest put together a team of Earhart, pilot Bill Stultz, and mechanic

Lou "Slim" Gordon. Amelia was not the main flyer, but more of a navigational assistant. It was Guest's goal merely to get a woman across the Atlantic by flight, not necessarily to have one flying solo.

In those times, flight across the Atlantic Ocean took off from the easternmost point of Canada. Those planes had limited fuel capacities, even the ones modified to carry extra gas like the Fokker. The planes flew north and refueled in Nova Scotia or Newfoundland before they were ferried to the airfield chosen for official departure to Europe. Earhart's team left from Trepassy, Newfoundland.

Bad weather hindered the start, delaying takeoff, and several aborted takeoffs kept the Fokker on the ground longer than expected be- fore the trio finally took off in the turbulent, foggy air. Originally, the plane was bound for Paris, but the weather, and rapidly diminishing fuel stocks convinced Stultz that he had to find a place to land much sooner.

As the plane burst free of the clouds on the outskirts of the European continent, the gas tank indicator was hovering near empty. They were approaching Ireland—the most appealing landing spot—and a large ship was in sight beneath them. It was depressing to realize that after all of the hard work they might fail to reach their destination and risk their lives in the water. Fearful of running out of gas, the flyers wrote a note and Amelia dropped it out of a plane in a bag weighted down with two oranges. The idea was to alert the captain that they might have to ditch in the water and need an emergency pickup. However, the note plummeted into the sea unnoticed.

The flyers knew if they kept circling the ship and spent more time trying to attract its attention they would simply use up more fuel. They gambled and flew onward, towards land. When they saw some small fishing boats they theorized they were not far from a harbor and a community. They hoped to quickly spy the coastline and a possible landing area. Luckily, the plane was equipped with pontoons that allowed them to land on water. They just needed to find somewhere to land their plane where it would not destroyed by waves or rocks

Stultz found a spot to land the plane, but it was in the water just offshore of Wales, located east of Ireland and west of England. They had achieved their goal of flying across the Atlantic, a task completed in twenty hours and forty minutes. But no one immediately knew what they had done because their radio was broken. The small number of people around had no idea who they were. In a humorous scene, Amelia waved to some men and one man took off his coat and waved back.

Finally, the fishing boats approached and the flyers were taken ashore in Burry Point, Wales. Once their accomplishment became known, Amelia, Stultz, and Gordon became a sensation, with thousands of people mobbing them. Overnight, they became international celebrities.

The group flew southeast to Southampton, England, meeting up with Amy Guest for festivities that were beginning everywhere. Mostly, it was celebrating Amelia, even though she tried to credit the men. She was well aware that she was not the main pilot, but the glow of being the first woman to cross the ocean by air shed a brilliant light on her.

Though Amelia was part of a team,
she was the most celebrated of the flight
in both Europe and the United States

At this point in her life, Amelia was doing things mostly because she wanted to, not for any type of recognition or reward. She truly did not expect the level of attention produced by this flight. It changed her life forever.

A parade was held in New York City
to celebrate Amelia's trans-Atlantic flight
and people lined the streets to see her

In England, Amelia met royalty and there
were parades for her. She accepted big-money
deals ($10,000) to write her story for the *New
York Times* and the *London Times*. The rich and
famous wanted to meet her. After this all-

conquering stay in England, the same type of
reception greeted Amelia (and the others) in New York. They returned to America
on a boat captained by Harry Manning.
Before Amelia left the Denison House for

Amelia poses for photographs with
her teammates Bill Stultz and Lou (Slim) Gordon
just after their successful flight

a two week vacation, she had not told anyone of the historic flight she was attempting. Her coworkers thought she was reading books at the beach. The spectacularly acclaimed journey kept her away for a bit of extra time. When Amelia returned to Boston, she was greeted by an incredible gathering of 250,000 people. From there, Amelia was whisked around the country. She was even given the key to the city in Pittsburgh. The transatlantic trio of Stultz, Earhart, and Gordon came back together in Williamsburg, Pennsylvania, to visit pilot Stultz's hometown. And then Amelia stopped in at her old high school in Chicago.

That whirlwind journey was followed by hiding out at Putnam's home. He was married at the time, and Amelia and Dorothy Putnam became good friends. They started to record the journey and write a book on Amelia's experiences. Due to her success, Amelia soon became aviation editor of *Cosmopolitan* magazine, a women's magazine that published articles of public interest.

Amelia took on assignments promoting aviation, many aimed at convincing women to look into related careers. She met and appeared at events with Charles Lindbergh and his wife Anne Morrow Lindbergh.

Three of the pilots in the first Women's Air Derby in 1929 smile after a successful race

Generous by nature, this trait spilled over to her work advocating for other women pilots. She encouraged others to fly and argued, sometimes verbally, sometimes in print, on behalf of female flyers whom she felt were discriminated against by the industry or by men in positions of power. When a Women's Air Derby was founded, Amelia felt she must be part of it, even if she didn't think she had the speedy equipment to win. She loudly championed women's rights to keep such an event going and blustered against anyone who felt women did not have the skills to race at high speed.

Putnam was almost always by Earhart's side, her one-man publicity machine smoothing the way on travels and lining up new and lucrative deals that kept her in the public eye and made her money. Amelia had always intended to resume working at Denison House since she loved her social work job, but the developments following the flight in the Fokker vastly increased her earning power, and the power of her voice on aviation matters.

Circumstances and events had created an exciting, on-the-go lifestyle for Amelia. Following the triumph of the 1928 flight across the Atlantic Ocean, Amelia Earhart was no longer a social worker. She was fully identified in the public mind as an aviator.

Chapter 5
<u>Accomplishments</u>

Life became a social whirl for Amelia Earhart. She wrote a book and aviation articles for magazines, was invited to major events, and posed for photo shoots. Amelia began endorsing products such as cars, airline luggage, and more. By endorsing these products, she earned even more money. She also became a popular lecturer and, in her talks, always promoted aviation and encouraged women to embrace careers outside of the home. She also wrote to encourage people

Amelia endorsed various products, like cars, which gave her even more influence and fame

to be open to the idea of flight in general as either pilots or just passengers.

In 1929, partially at Amelia's request, a group of female pilots gathered and created The Ninety-Nines, an association of women pilots formed to share interests and lobby for worthy issues. Eventually, Earhart became the first president of the association, which continues as an international organization today.

In 1929, Amelia helped found the group of female pilots called the Ninety-Nines

It was a constant theme for Amelia to inspire women to resist the limitation of being only housewives and mothers. She encouraged them to fulfill their professional potential if they so desired. She declined marriage because she did not want to be placed "in a cage," as she put it, until George Putman and his wife divorced and he repeatedly proposed to Amelia. She finally accepted—but with conditions.

George Putnam, after asking repeatedly, finally gets Amelia to agree to marry him in 1931

Her rules for marriage meant that Putnam could not boss her around and could not require her to stay home. Amelia wished to fly free, literally and figuratively, and continue to pursue her aviation career. Putnam agreed and was usually alongside her when she prepared for journeys or made trips, serving as a middle man by arranging most of them.

Finally flying her own plane again,
Amelia set many new records for women
in altitude and speed with her Lockheed Vega 5B

Amelia obtained a Lockheed Vega 5B, a new plane, and periodically set speed and altitude records for women. In 1932, Amelia became determined to pluck the most coveted of flying records still available. She wished to become the first woman to fly solo across the Atlantic Ocean. Five years had passed since Charles Lindbergh broke the barrier, and several other women had failed to replicate the flight. Earhart had won fame for flying across the ocean in a plane piloted by someone else, but now she wanted to do it by herself.

No announcement was made public of Amelia's goal, and frenzied preparations were made in secret. The finest navigators and mechanics were enlisted to modify her plane. Amelia dressed in her usual pilot's garb, but did not pack additional clothing. For refreshment, she took along tomato juice, her favorite beverage, and a thermos of soup. Once again the takeoff point was designated as Newfoundland, this time Harbor Grace.

In the days leading up to the departure, Amelia did something a little out of the ordinary, staying calm and relying on husband George as her manager to obtain weather reports and let her know the coast was clear for a safe flight. Few people knew what she was up to—it was her choice to limit publicity. She didn't want other women to jump ahead of her and, if things went haywire and she couldn't take off, it might be a less-publicized failure.

Weather reports were favorable enough to fly on May 20, and Amelia set her course. She planned to follow Lindbergh's route to Paris. Her flight was not to be so free and easy, however. Pilots preferred night flying and Amelia took off into the darkness with the belief that the sighted storms were to the south. Initially, visibility was grand and, from as high as 12,000 feet, Earhart could see icebergs in the ocean.

But soon her altimeter—the gadget that let her know how high she was flying—broke. After that it was up to Amelia to figure out how high above the water she was. A few hours into the trip, Amelia sniffed burning oil. There was a tiny fire from a broken part and momentarily she considered turning back to Newfoundland, but she flew onward. An hour or so later the storm she believed she was evading struck the plane.

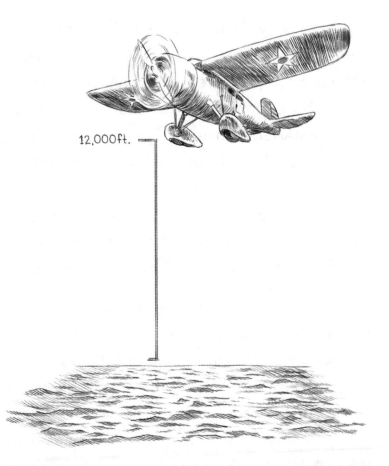

12,000ft.

Amelia relied on her altimeter to tell her how far from the water she was

Amelia flew in thick, black clouds and heavy rain that then turned to ice. As the controls froze up, the plane began to lose control. Amelia dropped so low that warmer air melted the ice, but she nearly flew into high ocean waves.

It took very skillful and careful flying to continue safely and to find a balance of the right altitude that prevented icing, yet kept Amelia safely above the water. Once that crisis passed, another started. When she turned to her reserve tanks of gasoline, she discovered a leak, and gas dripped down upon her head and neck. It was no wonder that the desire to land in France, on Lindbergh's old turf, was abandoned in favor of seeking the first handy strip of European land.

After fourteen hours and fifty-six minutes in the air, Amelia landed her plane in a field near Londonderry, Northern Ireland. No one knew she was coming, and no one knew who she was when she climbed out of the plane. There were more cows than humans in the vicinity at first. When one of a few farm workers there asked if Amelia had flown far, she replied simply,

"From America." The peace and quiet that enveloped her on that lonely patch of ground did not last long. Once word spread that the first woman had flown the Atlantic on her own, the excitement was even greater than that which surrounded Amelia on her first flight with Bill Stultz and Lou Gordon.

People cheered Amelia for being
the first woman to cross the Atlantic by herself

Already a major celebrity, Amelia Earhart's fame was greatly magnified by this latest achievement. The United States Congress awarded her the Distinguished Flying Cross. The French government presented Amelia with the Cross of a

Knight of the Legion of Honor. The National Geographic Society rewarded Amelia with its gold medal which was presented by President Herbert Hoover.

Once again, Amelia was celebrated and honored by kings, queens, statesmen, and adoring crowds of people. Amelia's first book was so well-received that, under George Putnam's guidance, she wrote another book describing the details of her solo trip. Appropriately, given her attitude towards the entire aviation experience, the second book was named, *The Fun of It*.

Now she was even more popular than ever. Amelia had fans in high places and fans in all places. She actively wrote aviation stories and made speeches in towns across America. One year she gave 136 speeches.

Amelia never seemed to run out of energy and made her demanding travel schedule easier by flying herself between communities on many occasions. She treated herself to a new airplane, a newer Vega, and painted it red with gold stripes. It was a toss-up whether or not it was as colorful as that old yellow car she called the canary, but Amelia was certain that it was a beautiful sight silhouetted against white clouds.

Amelia published her second book, *The Fun of It*, about flying across the Atlantic solo

Earhart had the gift of making friends easily and found it easy to talk in public. For her time, she was very much the independent woman who announced radical or new thoughts. It is difficult for young people of today to believe that in the 1930s women were not supposed to dream of having jobs outside their homes and that most were even discouraged from attending college. Society defined their roles as being wives and mothers who stayed at home all day to cook and clean.

Amelia became a regular public speaker and always tried to speak about women's rights when she could

Amelia was honest and truthful in her lectures, newspaper interviews, and articles about very actively discouraging that type of thought. Certainly, she said, it was okay to be a wife and mother, but that shouldn't be the be-all of a sophisticated, intelligent lady's existence. It was alright to want more and to test oneself in other ways. Amelia often said that she knew of many boys who were better suited to bake cakes than to fly planes and that many women were better suited to be aviators than stay-at-home cooks.

Amelia's prominent visibility gave her access to some of the most influential people in the United States. One of her biggest fans was Eleanor Roosevelt, the First Lady and wife of President Franklin D. Roosevelt. FDR was elected to the first of his four terms as President in 1932, and Eleanor loved aviation. She wanted to take flying lessons herself, but the president did not think it was an appropriate activity for her.

Eleanor and Amelia became good friends, though. One evening, after a formal dinner at the White House, Amelia asked Eleanor if she had ever flown at night. Eleanor responded that she had not and the two women, dressed in gowns, went to a nearby airport. They flew around Washington, D.C. and Amelia showed off the lights of the nation's capital city. The First Lady was giddy with excitement from the memorable flight.

The two women remained fast friends and it was a friendship that proved fruitful later. It provided Amelia with access to the president when aviation-related issues took center stage in America. And when she needed assistance in years to come, the door to the Oval Office, where the United States President worked, was open to Amelia.

Eleanor Roosevelt was one of Amelia's biggest fans and frequently invited her to dine at the White House

Chapter 6
<u>Fame</u>

In the 1930s, an era without television or the Internet, Amelia Earhart was fabulously famous. She was written about in newspapers and magazines, and she made a huge number of public appearances. Growing up, her family had to worry about money. Not anymore. This was in a time when many people were struggling to earn money. When her father died, she paid his medical bills. She generously helped support her mother and sister too.

The Great Depression hit people hard and Amelia gave them something to hope for

Amelia dressed nicely, choosing her fashions carefully. Then she began designing her own clothes and selling them in shops. She did not wish to own expensive appliances, and she could afford to fly anywhere she wanted in her own plane.

She became a spokeswoman for various airline ventures, always talking up the value of commercial air travel, and directed many of her ads and comments at women. Although her fondness for Denison House never waned, her life had become too busy for the tasks of a social worker. She was constantly on the go.

A chance meeting at a luncheon helped redirect Amelia's professional world, and ultimately, her entire life. In 1934, Earhart was seated next to a gentleman named Edward Elliott, who was president of Purdue University in West Lafayette, Indiana. Elliott was very impressed by Amelia and was taken with her message about women working outside the home.

Her talk that day meshed with his own goals for his school. Elliott believed that college educations were important for young women so they could hold good jobs in the workforce. He believed that education could give women the same career opportunities as men. Elliott offered Amelia a job at his college and, although she was not trained to be a university professor, she accepted the position and moved to the central Indiana campus.

Purdue University president, Edward Elliott, hired Amelia to encourage women to attend his university and continue their schooling after high school

Although Amelia did not have the qualification to be a professor, Elliott had a grander use for her talents in mind. Elliott knew that Earhart could inspire young women. That might not be a course for credit, but both of them thought it was a worthwhile project for society.

There was opposition to this vision on campus amongst faculty members and other officials. Everyone clearly did not share the goal of training women to think for themselves, delay marriage, and engage in careers. Amelia was a controversial person at Purdue, sometimes simply because she often chose to wear pants rather than skirts.

Amelia taught students at
Purdue University about aerodynamics

In spite of negative opinions, however, Amelia gave daily talks and lectures, and female students flocked to hear her, ate up what she said, and listened carefully to her recommendations and life experience. She had lived the lifestyle she was endorsing. Although Earhart did not finish college, she had experienced some post-high school education, had built her own career, and had not gotten married until she was established and past the age of thirty.

Amelia was very happy with her assignment. She very much enjoyed talking to the young women. There was no phrase in use at the time that referred to women's liberation, and nobody referred to such goings-on as a mass movement, but Amelia was ahead of her time in advocating the positions she took. In later years, her views would become common across the country.

Whether she was teaching young women, speaking to the public, or writing about aviation, thoughts of making her own flights were never far out of Amelia's mind. During the first half of the 1930s, Amelia set seven different women's records for speed or distance traveled in an airplane. She competed in the Bendix Trophy Race, although her plane was not built to go as fast as some of her competitors' planes.

Amelia took off from Hawaii's Wheeler Field for her record-breaking flight from Hawaii to California, a 2,400 mile trip

Amelia got the most pleasure out of flying her own plane to specific destinations. In 1935, she became the first person to fly the 2,400 miles between Hawaii and California solo, across the Pacific Ocean. Amelia flew this route with extreme appreciation for the beauty of the sky. She reflected, "It was a night of stars, of tropic loveliness. Stars hung outside my cockpit window near enough to touch."

The trip was supported financially by Hawaiian business people who wanted to promote tourism to the islands. Essentially, those business people wanted to show Americans that such a trip could be done.

By flying that route, Amelia became the first person to fly over both the Atlantic and Pacific oceans.

When she landed in Oakland, California, there were 10,000 people there cheering for her. A few months later, Amelia became the first person to fly solo from Los Angeles to Mexico City. She landed in Mazatlan, Mexico covering a distance of 1,000 miles.

Upon leaving Mexico, Amelia flew 700 miles across the Gulf of Mexico and eventually onward to Newark, New Jersey for a total journey of 2,080 miles. This was also a new solo flying record. All of these adventures kept Earhart in the news. At either the beginning or end of her journeys, George Putnam was around to encourage and support her and help her cope with the attention. He had his own personal nickname for her, calling her "A.E."

President Elliott did everything he could to make Amelia's stay at Purdue a successful one. He liked the attention her presence and involvement brought to the school, as well as the way she helped him accomplish the mission he had set out for women. The circumstances were very challenging for Elliott. The university endured budget cuts coming out of the Great Depression, yet Elliott spared no expense for Amelia.

The ultimate signal of Elliot's cooperation with Amelia was the school investing $80,000 for a Lockheed Electra that was called a "flying laboratory" designed for aviation research. Purchased under the umbrella of the Purdue Research Foundation, the airplane was pretty much only for Earhart's use. It was delivered on July 24, 1936, Amelia's 39th birthday. It was just about the best birthday present she could imagine.

There were plans to perform scientific studies related to flight. Amelia wanted this laboratory to find out how flying affected certain people at high altitude, and how what a person ate before flying could affect his or her body. She was curious if there were any differences between how men and women reacted to flying, and whether or not the number of cockpit instruments created weariness in a pilot.

All of this was worthy of praise and could be scientifically useful. Some people seemed offended that so much money was being spent on an airplane for Amelia to play with, as they saw

Amelia planned a large variety of experiments to do while flying the Lockheed Electra

it. But she actually did have another secret plan in mind for what she wanted to do with it.

When Amelia first took flying lessons she learned in a very fragile biplane. This new Lockheed was quite sturdy. While not a jet propelled aircraft like today's models, the Lockheed was similar because it had the streamlined body of one. The two engines were propeller-driven, but they were much stronger than the older ones. Technology had come a long way in a short time. There were no more open cockpits either, where the pilots had to endure wind and rain.

Mostly using a plane for her personal transportation flying city-to-city, Amelia had made all of the big, first flights she had as goals. But there was one exception. Amelia always wanted to show that women could do what men could do. She had one more magnificent flight challenge in mind to accomplish. Amelia Earhart dreamed of becoming the first woman to pilot an airplane around-the-world.

Chapter 7
Record-Breaking Plans

The first airplane flight around-the-world was a unique undertaking. Four planes were outfitted identically for four different pilots and the men departed from Seattle on April 6, 1924. The flyers were all military men: Major Frederick Martin, Lt. Lowell H. Smith, First Lt. Leigh P. Wade, and Lt. Erik Nelson. The U.S. Navy deposited thirty replacement engines around the world for possible use.

Also, the Navy, with the help of the Royal Air Force, placed barrels of fuel at strategic locations. One plane got lost in fog and crashed in Alaska, but the other three planes completed the flight of 25,810 miles. It took the men until the end of September to complete the trip.

What Amelia Earhart was hoping to do had been accomplished by men, but she was always proud to take on challenges that women had never had the opportunity to try. With her new Lockheed Electra, Amelia thought she had a plane that was powerful enough, with some modifications, to make a successful flight.

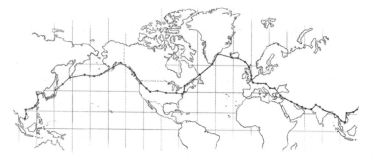

The route the four US Navy officers
flew around the world

Her goal was to fly the plane around the earth at its widest point, crossing the equator. If all went according to plan, the flight would cover an estimated 27,000 plus miles. This was not one of Amelia's pioneering flights that would be attempted solo. She was definitely in the market for a highly intelligent navigator.

Although she and George Putnam wished to keep the news quiet about her attempt, some word was leaked so they could interview and investigate the best possible available navigator. Studying maps and consulting experts,

Amelia and George settled on a route. The original idea was for Amelia to take off from Oakland, California and fly to Hawaii, then to a little-known island in the Pacific Ocean called Howland Island. From there she would fly to Australia, Arabia, Africa, Brazil in South America, and then back to the United States.

After careful consideration, the navigator chosen was Harry Manning. Amelia had known him since 1928. Manning was captain of the ship that brought her back to America after her celebratory visit in England following her first

Harry Manning, Amelia's friend, helped her plan her flight and stops around the world

flight across the Atlantic. A third person, Fred Noonan, was added to the crew, and would offer relief services, if needed. A fourth member of the group was mechanic Paul Mantz, who made sure all the parts were in tip-top shape. He planned to fly as far as Hawaii to meet up with his fiancée.

The main challenge facing Amelia and the crew was flying across the Pacific Ocean. The distance was too great to cover without a refueling stop. Where exactly to take on that fuel was not an easy choice to make. There would only be tiny islands, many of them uninhabited. From the sky, the islands would look like tiny dots on the vast ocean.

This is where Amelia's close personal friendship with Eleanor Roosevelt, who admired her greatly, and President Roosevelt paid off. Her worldwide fame did not hurt her cause, either. The Navy was looking to develop a refueling stop in the Pacific and it was tentatively colonizing Howland Island with a small number of people for a base. Amelia's pull and influence resulted

President Roosevelt and Eleanor helped Amelia's trip by building her a refueling stop at Howland Island

in a fast construction of a refueling center that she could use on this critical leg of the journey. It was an expensive proposition, but the president's power helped Amelia's needs.

The schedule called for a March 17, 1937 take-off from Oakland, California. As it so happened, it was a rainy day, but the weather was not bad enough to ground Amelia. The sixteen-hour flight to Hawaii went smoothly. The weather was bad there and kept the Electra on the runway for a couple of days. On March 20, Amelia revved the engine, steered the plane forward, and it did not lift off the ground. Instead the plane swerved left, the landing gear collapsed, and a wing was damaged. Gasoline began leaking.

There were no human injuries, but the plane suffered mightily, and the repairs required ended the flight. It was estimated that everything would be on hold for two months. Frustrated with the circumstances, Amelia resolved to be patient and try again. However, the delay resulted in one major problem for the overall plan. Manning was on a leave of absence from his job, but had to go back to work and could not join the others on the re-try. It was to be Earhart and Noonan all the way.

But, the weather patterns were different in March than in May. This meant it was much safer to fly around-the-world in the opposite direction.

Due to the delay, the crew ended up only being
Amelia and Fred Noonan

All supplies of gasoline and spare parts needed to be restocked, and new maps and charts would be needed. Instead of flying from California to Hawaii and then refueling at Howland Island right away, Amelia would fly most of the way around-the-world and approach Howland near the end of the adventure.

Since Amelia had already flown across the United States as a solo pilot, she decided not to announce her trip until she got to Miami, Florida. In Miami, her attempt was publicly announced just before she left for the first international stop on the trip, San Juan, Puerto Rico.

A key aspect in the pre-planning was to ensure that Amelia and Noonan knew a sufficient amount about handling the radios, and a recent innovation in navigation called a direction finder that could be very helpful in bad weather. Everyone also assumed that both were proficient in Morse Code as a standby, the signaling system by telegraph with which they could send messages, even if their voices could not be heard. For extra range on the radio, Mantz made sure the plane was equipped with a wire trailing antenna that, when let out, was two hundred and fifty feet long. Amelia did not like the process of reeling the antenna in and out, but Mantz insisted that the value was worth it to help radio reception.

The telegraph key was used to transmit Morse Code, which would spell out messages through a series of dots and dashes

Takeoff was set for June 1st. An early start was planned and Amelia was in the cockpit by 5 a.m. Husband George leaned in the window for some private words and to wish his wife well. When Amelia and Noonan flew off into the wild blue yonder, the trailing antenna and a telegraph key for Morse Code were not with them. Amelia apparently had exiled the equipment from the plane.

Chapter 8
Around-the-World

The grand journey was underway and the first leg complete when Amelia Earhart and Fred Noonan set down in Puerto Rico to spend the night. The clear flying meant that at times Amelia could put the plane on auto-pilot. When that occurred, Amelia spent her time taking notes instead of steering.

She had a contract to write newspaper articles for *The New York Herald-Tribune* and send them in whenever the plane landed and re-contacted with civilization. She also kept a broader diary and those notes were intended for use later at home, when she collected the articles and additional notes into a book.

Interestingly, it was easier for Amelia to write things down than to talk to Noonan, who sat only a few feet from her. That was because the cockpit was so noisy. At times, Noonan retreated to the rear of the plane. When he was in the back

When the plane was on auto-pilot,
Amelia journaled for the *New York Herald-Tribune*
as well as her future book

cabin, he attached hand-written notes for Amelia
at the end of a bamboo fishing pole. Legend has
it that these handwritten notes were the only way
the two communicated during flight. The fishing
pole was only needed, however, when Noonan
left his seat up front.

Flying out of Puerto Rico, the duo flew south
to Venezuela and then went southeast and
stopped in Dutch Guiana, which is modern day
Suriname. The next stop was southbound to

Brazil. Although they were partners in this ambitious journey, Amelia and Noonan did not know each other well before takeoff. They became good friends as they flew and shared the experience.

The two-person crew and the plane were doing fine. The plane was serviced, gassed up, and was readied for a long, 1,900-mile overseas flight from Brazil in South America to Senegal in Africa. The destination was the city of Dakar, at the time governed by the French, which is now the capital of Senegal. They approached in a dense haze, and they had difficulty seeing the right place to land. This obstacle made their landing less than precise—they were off by fifty miles to the north, landing in St. Louis, Senegal instead.

Sometimes Amelia and Fred spent a day or two on break during their stopovers, but they were conscious of making time and sometimes just grabbed a night's sleep and were on their way again. Senegal was a quick break. The next day they began their flight across the continent of Africa, 4,500 miles with periodic, planned stops.

Amelia and Fred were amazed by the rhinoceroses
and lions near the landing strip in Sudan

At modern American airports, sometimes jets
are thrown off by large flocks of birds. In some
places, deer or moose hang around the runways.
When Amelia and Fred approached the African
Sudan, they noticed that there was an eight foot
tall hedge thick with thorns that kept out lions
and rhinoceroses.

When planning this mission Amelia and her
helpful organizers had to contact the officials in
various countries to make sure the plane would
gain permission to set down in these foreign
lands. Some diplomacy was needed to gain all
of the approvals and in one case landing rights

were denied. Fred and Amelia were shut out of Saudi Arabia by the authorities.

When they left Africa behind, they had a 2,000 mile trip to Karachi, Pakistan. Amelia noted that this trip resembled the pretend journeys she took in her childhood.

Decades ago it became a popular stereotype for those on vacation to write postcards to loved ones with the simple message, "Wish you were here." It became a joke, more or less, to send those. However, in Karachi Amelia did send a message to her husband saying that precise thing.

Then, the Earhart-Noonan team flew southeast 1,390 miles to Calcutta, India, where they encountered heavy rains. They had run into the monsoon season. The runway was a muddy mess and they did not stay long, taking off east as soon as possible for Burma, now known as Myanmar.

But as Amelia and Fred flew along, the storm stripped paint off of the plane. After two hours, they had to turn back and start over the next day. After Rangoon, Burma, it was 1,200 miles to Singapore, and then on to the Netherlands East Indies, now known as Indonesia.

Sometimes fierce weather kept them in one place longer than initially planned. Once in a while, mechanical fine-tuning was needed for the plane. But by the end of June, the duo was in Port Darwin, Australia.

Amelia's journal writings kept Americans excited about the flight. One of the toughest legs began in Port Darwin after they cut weight by shipping home all equipment they could. Amelia and Fred had to fight headwinds, and it took nearly eight hours to fly east and reach Lae, New Guinea.

They had completed 22,000 miles, but the team faced the riskiest segment of the entire trip. They were going to fly across the Pacific Ocean, and the key to their success was refueling on Howland Island.

When Amelia was asked how big Howland Island was, she made a circle with her thumb and forefinger on her right hand that seemed to approximate the size of a quarter. That was an exaggeration, but it made the point that she and Noonan were going to search for a small area of land amidst a vast ocean of turbulent water.

Amelia flew from Port Darwin, Australia to Lae, New Guinea and then on to Howland Island

Howland Island was southwest of Hawaii, and while there were other small islands in the area, it was really the only target Amelia and Fred had. Few of the other islands had people living on them, and none of them had fuel. Leaving Lae, Earhart and Noonan had between

5,000 and 7,000 miles to fly to finish their adventure around-the-world.

The United States government had been very helpful to the flyers. The Coast Guard cutter ship *Itasca* was assigned to stand-by near Howland Island for several purposes. Its general assignment was to patrol the area, but now it was available to track Amelia's incoming plane and communicate by radio, helping the pilot and navigator find their way to the ground. In case of emergency, *Itasca* was also on the scene to help.

The Coast Guard sent the *Itasca* to help Amelia and Fred land on the right island

It was mid-morning on July 2, 1937 when Amelia and Fred gunned the engine of the Electra and took off from New Guinea on their way to Howland Island. Although weather reports were often unreliable and unpredictable at the time, no bad weather was anticipated. The fuel load should have been sufficient for more than twenty-one hours.

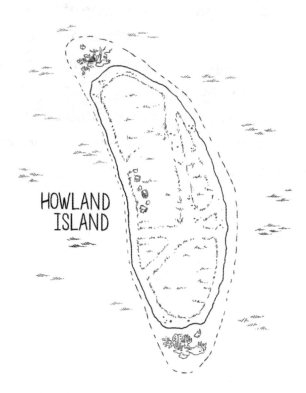

HOWLAND
ISLAND

Howland Island was a small island
and home only to a few airstrips

Chapter 9
Lost Flight

Amelia Earhart and Fred Noonan had covered 22,000 miles by air by the time they left New Guinea, having made thirty stops in nineteen countries on five continents as they navigated towards Howland Island in the Pacific Ocean.

Howland Island is two miles long and a half mile wide and is twenty feet above sea level. It was a patch of land that could easily be missed despite meticulous planning. A Navy ship called the *USS Ontario* was midway between Lae and Howland and was positioned to relay weather updates to the plane. The *Itasca*, the Coast Guard cruiser stationed off-shore, was supposed to offer aid in finding Howland Island and pick up radio signals once the plane reached the area.

There were other small islands in the general vicinity also, Nauru and the Great Britain-owned Gilbert Islands. As the plane passed near Nauru, Amelia did have radio communication with the ground. Warner Thompson, commander of the *Itasca*, was alerted that the plane was headed in his direction.

After that, things went horribly wrong. The *Itasca* sent out signals, but no official communications with the plane were ever made. From this point on, no one has ever been able to figure out precisely what happened. There was very clearly a huge miscommunication between plane and ship. No direct voice contact was made. Shortwave radios have their own special transmission frequencies separate from AM or FM radio. Those channels pick up radio waves that are reflected back to earth from the ionosphere, which is a layer of the earth's atmosphere. That helps the signal to follow the curve of the planet, allowing for communications to travel much farther.

Those on the *Itasca* didn't even realize that Amelia was not alone, and any time they heard a faint SOS from a male voice, they concluded the call could not be coming from the plane they were seeking to locate. The two transportation vehicles

were never on the same wavelength—literally
missing signals in radio contact.

A typical shortwave radio receiver of the day

People on the ship repeatedly sent Morse
Code messages, but Amelia and Fred did not
have their telegraph key and didn't have enough
knowledge of it anyway. As hours passed, the
sailors frantically sought to communicate with
the plane, but it was impossible. There were
strange and sporadic reports from shortwave
radio connections thousands of miles away of
Amelia's voice calling for help.

Amelia's voice was heard on radios in
Wyoming, Texas, and Florida, and where home

short-wave antennas had been greatly enhanced to create virtual super radios. Authorities did not follow up with these people because the listeners were teenagers, and their locations seemed so far away from Howland Island. It is likely that these young people heard the last pleas of the missing flyers.

Once those aboard the *Itasca* determined that the plane was so late it must have run out of fuel, a search was instigated. Some reports indicated that the Coast Guard ship acted on incorrect information and made poor assumptions. It was also hampered by lack of communication and miscommunication. The ship sailed around and around searching, often without valid reasons for its directional choices.

Newspaper reporters deployed in different places began sending messages to the United States that Amelia Earhart and Fred Noonan did not land on time and had been reported missing. This provoked sensational attention across the country. No one was more alarmed or worried than George Putnam, Amelia's husband, who was in regular contact with Navy officials and sought constant reassurance that all was being done to find the flyers.

It was reported that Earhart and Noonan were carrying a rubber lifeboat aboard, but in reality they were not. Everyone believed they could be reached by Morse Code, but they could not. While it made sense to concentrate search resources near Howland, as time passed and that area was checked, more ships and planes reached the area and spread out over wider distances, believing that the flight was off-course.

No one really knew, though. The reason that this around-the-world flight shaped up as such a challenge in the first place was the tremendous open areas of ocean surrounding small islands like Howland. Now that issue was a huge problem. There was too much water and too little land.

The plane could have crashed into the sea and disappeared completely. The plane could have overshot its mark by one hundred miles and been off to the north, or to the south, east, or west.

Amelia and Fred could have crash-landed on an uninhabited island and been marooned in the middle of nowhere, injured, with nothing to eat. All of this was speculation.

Hours passed with no official word from the plane. Night became day. No word. Days passed with not a single clue to guide the planes and ships scouring the region for a trace of Amelia, Fred, or the plane. No debris was seen floating on the surface of the water.

Newspapers announced Amelia and Fred's disappearance across the country, heightening the concern

More time passed and the search expanded, and Navy planes began checking out the other small islands in the region. Mostly, they flew overhead and when they saw no sign of life they checked off the island as void of people. Other islands that were inhabited were checked, but no one reported seeing Amelia or Fred or the plane.

Later, one of the rumor-hoax stories that sprung up was that Amelia and Fred had crashed on the Japanese-controlled Marshall Islands, were taken prisoner, and charged as spies. Or that they spent years living in captivity before

Amy Earhart was devastated
by her daughter's disappearance

dying in secret. No credibility was attached to those stories, but the United States did check with the Japanese government during this time period before World War II to see if any sign of the missing aviators was noted.

As the world held its breath, and as George Putnam retained his faith, the search went on for sixteen days. Yet no hint of what fate held for Amelia Earhart and Fred Noonan was ever discovered.

Amelia was survived by her sister Muriel, a former teacher in Boston, and a poet with a master's degree from Harvard. Deeply saddened by her older sister's disappearance, in later years she wrote a poem dedicated to Amelia, and in 1963 published a biography of her called *Courage is the Price*. Amelia was also out-lived by her mother, Amy, who reacted to her disappearance by publically calling it "a great loss."

For decades there have been searches and theories as to what actually happened to Amelia and Fred. As time moved on, the searches were conducted with improved and increasingly new technology, scientists, military officials and private citizens. Book after book has been written trying to answer the question of what went wrong for Amelia and Fred. Yet no definitive answer has ever been discovered, and no proof has ever been presented on where the plane went down.

Amelia earned her place on a United States postage stamp in 1963, an honor given to only a few American heroes

The story of Amelia Earhart and Fred Noonan's around-the-world flight of 1937 remains one of the great mysteries of American history.

Select Quotes from
<u>Amelia Earhart</u>

"The life of the mind, combined with a life of purpose and action..."

— *Earhart describing the way she hoped to live and contribute to society*

"There is no door closed to ability, so when women are ready there will be opportunity for them in aviation."

— *Earhart indicating that the world of aviation was not just a man's world*

"It was a night of stars, of tropic loveliness. Stars hung outside my cockpit window near enough to touch."

— *Earhart on the beauty of the night as she made the first solo flight from Honolulu, Hawaii to Oakland, California*

"It's a routine now. I make a record and then I lecture on it."

— *Earhart speaking about how her flying accomplishments created a way for her to make a living as a speaker*

Glossary

Air show   Pilots would perform tricks and stunts in their planes to amuse an audience

Altitude   Measurement of how high above sea level a person reaches, either in an airplane, or perhaps by climbing a mountain on foot

Atchison, Kansas   Community where Amelia Earhart was born in 1897

Biplane   Form of airplane in use during the early 1900s which featured a pair of wings, stacked one above the other, with the pilot's seat in-between

Caliber   The diameter of the gun barrel

Cockpit   Place where the pilot sits to fly the plane

Credit   When you buy something without money but with trust that you will pay the full amount later

Denison House   Live-in home for new immigrants in need located in Boston where Amelia Earhart was employed as a social worker

Distinguished Flying Cross   Intended as a military honor, the United States government bestowed the award on Amelia Earhart for her exploits as an aviation pioneer

Great Depression   The economic crisis and period of low business activity in the United States and other countries beginning with the stock-market crash in 1929 and continuing through most of the 1930s

Great Influenza Pandemic   In 1918, almost 30% of Americans caught the Spanish flu and over 20 million people died throughout the world

Howland Island   Small stretch of land in the Pacific Ocean where Amelia Earhart was attempting to land to refuel her plane on the flight around the world in 1937

Liberation   To set someone or something free from oppressive thought or imprisonment

Logbook   Official notes taken to describe the journey as an airplane or ship travels, usually kept by the captain, or a high ranking officer

Monsoon   Heavy rainfall or draught caused by seasonal wind change in southern parts of Asia

Morse Code   System of communication consisting of dots, dashes, spaces or sounds that substitute for letters, numbers and words, in sending messages by signals and clicks, transmitted by telegraph

Navigator   Person who helps a pilot guide the direction of an airplane or ship

Newfoundland   Canadian province that during the early days of Trans-Atlantic flight was used as the jumping-off point from North America to Europe because it was closer than such American cities as Boston and required the use of less fuel

The Ninety-Nines   First club for women pilots, founded by Amelia Earhart and some of her fellow aviators with Earhart as the first president

Purdue University   Major University located in Indiana that housed/supported Amelia Earhart, providing her with an $80,000 "flying laboratory" to do research on her flights

Short Wave Radio   Special type of radio that transmits via "short waves," sometimes carrying many hundreds of miles in distance beyond more traditional radios

Social Worker   Person who tries to help the less fortunate, the poverty-stricken, or others with disadvantages

Solo   When a person is the only one flying an airplane, without a crew

St. Louis World's Fair   Also called the Louisiana Purchase Exposition, the event held in St. Louis in 1904 was a spectacular fair many times bigger than a county or state fair

Transatlantic   Crossing the Atlantic Ocean

Transcontinental   Flying either from the West Coast of a continent to the East Coast, or from the East Coast to the West Coast

Women's Suffrage   Issue of providing women with the right to vote in political elections

World War I   Conducted on a worldwide scale between 1914 and 1918, this conflict was so terrible it was supposed to be "the war that ended all wars"

Amelia Earhart Timeline

1897 July 24   Born in Atchison, Kansas

1899 December 29   Sister Muriel is born

1909 September   Enrolls in public school, Des Moines, Iowa after being home-schooled, mostly by her grandparents

1917   Volunteers as a nurse in Toronto treating Canada's World War I injured soldiers

1919 September   Enrolls at Columbia University in New York City

1921 January 3   First flying lesson in California at age 23

1922 October 22   Set women's altitude record of 14,000 feet

1925   Sister Muriel marries Albert Morrissey

1925   Begins employment as a social worker at Denison House, Boston

1928 June 17-18   First woman on Trans-Atlantic flight

1929 November   Helps found and is first president of the Ninety-Nines

1930 September 23   Father dies

1931, February 7   Marries George Putnam

1932 May 20   First solo, non-stop Trans-Atlantic flight by a woman

World and Aviation Timeline

1897 March 4   United States President William McKinley is inaugurated

1903 December 17   The Wright Brothers, Orville and Wilbur, take off from Kitty Hawk, NC and travel one hundred and twenty feet in the first fixed-wing airplane flight

1909 July 25   Louis Bleriot makes the first flight across the English Channel and collects a prize of $10,000

1913 March 4   United States President Woodrow Wilson is inaugurated, serving to 1921

1914 January 1   Pilot Tony Jannus carries former St. Petersburg mayor Abraham C. Pheill to Tampa on the first-ever commercial flight

1914 July 28   World War I begins in Europe continuing until November 11, 1918

1917 April 6   United States enters World War I

1920 January 17   Federal legislation bans alcohol across the U.S. until 1933; this time period is known as "Prohibition"

1927 May 20-21   Flying from New York to Paris on a thirty-three hour trip, Charles Lindbergh completes the first solo non-stop Trans-Atlantic trip

1929 October   United States stock market crash begins triggering the years-long economic disaster called the Great Depression

1931 October 4-5   Clyde Pangborn and Hugh Herndon make the first non-stop flight across the Pacific Ocean from Japan to Wenatchee, Washington in forty-one hours, thirteen minutes

<u>Amelia Earhart Timeline</u> (cont.)

1932 August 24-25   Set woman's speed record flying across the U.S. from Los Angeles, California to Newark, New Jersey

1932   Writes *The Fun of It*

1935 January 11-12   First person to fly solo from Honolulu, Hawaii to Oakland, California, crossing the Pacific Ocean

1935 April 19-20   First person to fly solo from Los Angeles, California to Mexico City, Mexico

1935 Autumn   Joins faculty of Purdue University

1937 May 21   Leaves Oakland, California on the unofficial beginning of the around-the-world flight

1937 June 1   Start of around-the-world flight in Miami, Florida, traveled 22,000 miles

1937 July 2   Disappears while flying over the Pacific Ocean

1941 January 5   Declared dead after being missing since her airplane disappeared in 1937

World and Aviation Timeline (cont.)

1933 March 4   United States President Franklin Delano Roosevelt is inaugurated, serving until April 12, 1945

1937 May 3   Author Margaret Mitchell wins the Pulitzer Prize for writing *Gone with the Wind*

1937 May 28   First cars cross new Golden Gate Bridge in San Francisco

Bibliography

Butler, Susan. *East to the Dawn: The Life of Amelia Earhart*. Cambridge: Da Capo Press, 1997.

Fleming, Candace. *Amelia Lost: The Life and Disappearance of Amelia Earhart*. New York: Schwartz & Wade Books, 2011.

Gillespie, Ric. *Finding Amelia: The True Story of the Earhart Disappearance*. Annapolis: Naval Institute Press, 2006.

Lauber, Patricia. *Lost Star: The Story of Amelia Earhart*. New York: Scholastic, Inc., 1988.

Further Reading

Campbell, Mike. *Amelia Earhart: The Truth at Last*. Boiling Springs, PA: Sunbury Press, Inc., 2012.

Lovell, Mary. *The Sound of Wings: The Life of Amelia Earhart*. New York: St. Martins Press, 1989.

Rich, Doris L. *Amelia Earhart: A Biography*. Washington, DC: Smithsonian Institute Press, 1989.

Index